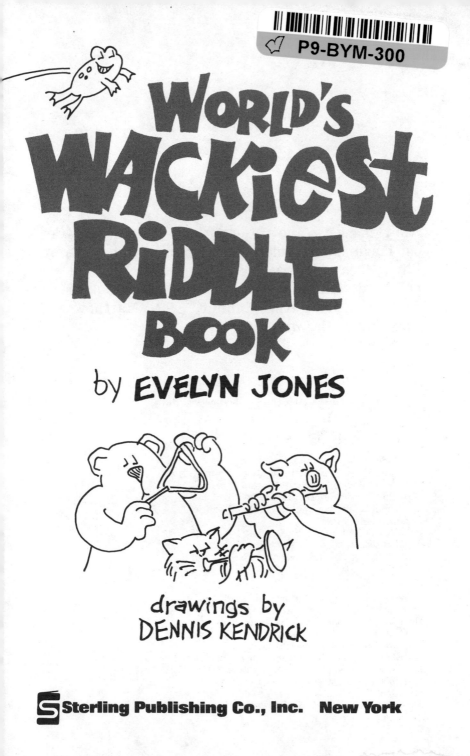

WORLD'S WACKIEST RIDDLE BOOK

by **EVELYN JONES**

drawings by
DENNIS KENDRICK

Sterling Publishing Co., Inc.   New York

*To Jeannie Colligan
and crazy conversation*

Many thanks to the patient friends on whom I tried out hundreds of riddles while writing this book: Amy, Phyl, Bucky, Sherry, Meredith, Donna Lee and her pupils at Stratham, N.H. Memorial School, Zach, Tom, Judy and Ann Rehner, Eric, Matthew and Christopher Brown.

Library of Congress Cataloging-in-Publication Data

Jones, Evelyn.
  World's wackiest riddle book.

  Includes index.
  Summary: An illustrated collection of hundreds of
riddles in categories such as "Fast & Freaky,"
"Pet Talk," and "Reverse Riddles."
  1. Riddles, Juvenile. [1. Riddles] I. Kendrick,
Dennis, ill. II. Title.
PN6371.5.J67 1986   818'.5402   86-5960
ISBN 0-8069-4736-5
ISBN 0-8069-4737-3 (lib. bdg.)

First Paperback Printing, 1987

CONTENTS

1. Fast & Freaky   5
2. All in a Day's Work   13
3. What's the Question?   25
4. Chewy Riddles   32
5. Pet Talk   41
6. Superstars & Other Greats   47
7. Mr. President, Mr. President!   55
8. Love & Hisses   58
9. Reverse Riddles   63
10. Animal Fare   71
11. Family Ties   85
12. Rhyme Time   90
13. Silly Gilly   93
14. The Cart Before the Horse   98
15. You Name It   106
16. People, Places & Things   109
17. Stumpers   119
    INDEX   126

• 1 •
FAST & FREAKY

Why do witches wear green eye shadow?
It matches their teeth.

Why did the witch buy a new bikini?
To enter the Mess America contest.

Why do witches carry cats on their broomsticks?
Because elephants get airsick.

What do little ghosts wear?
Pillowcases.

What color are they?
Boo!

What do little ghosts wear on their feet?
Boo-ties.

What game do they play?
Peek-a-BOO!

Where do little ghosts go swimming?
In Lake Eerie (Erie).

What kind of bats swing upside down?
Acro-bats.

What kind of bats know their ABC's?
Alpha-bats.

Why are demons always skinny?
They get lots of exorcise (exercise).

How do skeletons deliver the mail?
By Boney (Pony) Express.

What do you get if you cross a pony and a ghost?
Whinny the Boo.

The Joint Is Jumping

What do you get if you cross a bluejay and a frog?

The bluebird of hoppiness.

What happened to the frog who ate too much?

He turned into a hoppopotamus.

What happened to the frog who sat on a telephone?

He grew up to be a bellhop.

What happened to the frog who broke its leg?

It was hopless.

What does a frog use to build a house?

Toadstools (toad's tools).

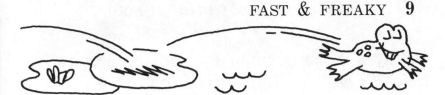

The Joint Is Jumping

How do Army frogs march?
"Hop, 2, 3, 4!"

Why did the frog get kicked out of
the Navy?
He kept jumping ship.

Why did the frog sit on the lily pad?
Her sofa was being repaired.

What happens when frogs get
married?
They live hoppily ever after.

Where do frogs go when they die?
To the hoppy hunting ground.

Why did the medium go into the hospital?
To have an apparition (operation).

What did the cannibal say to the missionary?
"Come for dinner."

What did the jelly say to the jam in heaven?
"Saints preserve us!"

What is the vampires' favorite city?
BOO-charest (Bucharest).

Where do the most annoying vampires go?
BOO-dapest (Budapest).

What's it like to eat breakfast with Scrooge?
It's a gruel-ing experience.

What does a witch put in her coffee?
Sugar and scream.

Why did Dracula visit an astrologer?
To get his horror-scope (horoscope).

What is Dracula's favorite food?
Hungarian ghoul-ash.

What is a mermaid's favorite food?
Peanut butter and jellyfish sandwich.

What little ghost lost its sheep?
Boo-Peep.

What did the ghoul use to wash its hair?
Sham-boo.

Why are Italian chefs so smart?
They always use their noodles.

What does a hungry giant order for lunch?
Ham on rhi-noceros!

What did the little vampire win in the Horribles Parade?
The BOO-by prize.

What did the little vampire say when they handed it the prize?
"Fang you!"

• 2 •
ALL IN A
DAY'S WORK

Why did the secret agent take two aspirins and go to bed?
He had a code in his head.

Why did the secret agent whisper "1, 2, 3, 4, 5, 6, 7 . . ."?
He was a counter-spy.

When does a lawyer make coffee?
When he has sufficient grounds.

Why did the judge send for a safecracker?
The jury was deadlocked.

Why did the judge send for a locksmith?
The key witness was missing.

Why was the calendar so sad?
Its days were numbered.

What's the difference between a girl who's
sick of her boyfriend and a sailor who falls in
the ocean?
*One is bored over a man and the other is
a man overboard.*

What color is bad luck for sailors?
Maroon.

Why is a tired soldier like a broken-down cathedral?
Both have fallen arches.

What happens when two Army officers collide?
It could be a Major disaster.

When do pilots fly close to the ground?
In so-low flights.

How does a train conductor sneeze?
"Ahhhh choo-choo!"

When does it get noisy in a magazine store?
When Time *marches on.*

Why did the carpenter hire a secretary?
To file his nails.

What kind of saws and nails are useless to a carpenter?
Seesaws and toenails.

What holds up a solar house?
Sunbeams.

Why did the prizefighter like his new job?
He got to punch the time clock.

What do you call a couple of salesmen who go to jail?
Sell-mates (cellmates).

What kind of people should never get wrapped up in their work?
The ones who raise boa constrictors.

Pure Corn

Why does a farmer think the letter R is amazing?
It can change a pea into a pear.

What did the farmer's wife raise in her living room?
The window.

What does a farmer do when he finds a hole in his garden?
He sows (sews) it.

What's the difference between a proud farmer and a pirate?
The farmer treasures his berries and the pirate buries his treasures.

How do grapes grow in California?
Just vine (fine), thanks.

Pure Corn

How does a farmer mend his overalls?
With cabbage patches.

When a ewe marries a ram, what does he become?
Her butt-er half.

When does a horse talk?
Whinny wants to.

What has four wheels and goes honk?
A goose on a skateboard.

When is mealtime in the henhouse?
Eggsactly six o'cluck.

Where in town do needleworkers live?
On the outskirts.

Why do dressmakers like the wide-open spaces?
So they don't feel hemmed in.

What did the stocking say to the needle?
"I'll be darned!"

What did the stocking say to the garter?
"Make it snappy; I gotta run."

Is it hard to learn to sew?
No, it's thimble (simple).

How did the teacher get locked out of the music room?

His keys were inside on the piano.

What kind of music can you play with a shoehorn?

Footnotes.

How does a musician brush his teeth?

With a tuba toothpaste.

When is a basketball player like a baby?

When he dribbles.

Are performing termites successful in the theatre?

Sure—they bring down the house!

When a couple of mice huddle in the back of a theatre, how cold is it?

Two below Z-row.

Why did the actor take his baseball bat to Times Square?

He wanted to make a hit on Broadway.

Why did the actor envy the artist?

The artist had no trouble drawing big crowds.

When is an absent-minded circus owner like a nervous actor?
When he forgets his lions (lines).

What happened when the magician did a scary trick?
His hare (hair) stood on end.

What happened when Miss Piggy appeared in a play?
She hogged the stage.

What did the critics say about her?
Never sausage (saw such) a ham!"

What did the lumberjack do after he cut down the tree?
He took a bough (bow).

Why can't Smokey go to the movies?
No one with bear (bare) feet is allowed.

What happens to King Kong when he works too hard?
He goes bananas.

What happens to Whistler's mother when she works too hard?
She goes off her rocker.

What happens to spoons when they work too hard?
They go stir crazy!

• 3 •
WHAT'S THE QUESTION?

In these great new riddles, you don't need to find the right answers. You get those to start with. What you need to find are the right questions! They're tough, but lots of fun. Try them on!

A: *Mount Vernon.*
Q: Before riding Vernon the horse, what must you do?

A: *7-Up.*
Q: What happens in Snow White's cottage when the alarm clock rings?

A: *Overlap.*
Q: Where is the belly button located?

A: *Tulips.*
Q: What's located beneath your nose?

A: *Overshoes.*
Q: Where are ankles located?

A: *Nose drops.*
Q: What happens when the bridge of your nose collapses?

A: *William Tell.*
Q: What does bigmouth William do when he hears a secret?

A: *Wilbur and Orville.*
Q: Name two people who were never wrong.

A: *Forebears.*
Q: Who are Paddington, Fozzie, Teddy and Smokey?

A: *Alienate.*
Q: What did E.T. do when he found a McDonald's?

A: *Marionette.*
Q: Has Marion had her breakfast?

A: *Radish.*
Q: If a green bean is greenish, what is a radish?

A: *Sandwich.*
Q: Who haunts the Sahara Desert?

A: *Harum-scarum.*
Q: Why doesn't the sheik get married?

A: *Dr. Pepper.*
Q: Who married Nurse Salt?

A: *Alligator.*
Q: I have a cat named Alec and a canary. Guess what happened.

A: *A Siberian husky.*
Q: Who won the Russian weight-lifting contest?

A: *Propaganda.*
Q: Who will Prim Goose go out with?

A: *Norwegian, Swede and Dane.*
Q: Name two Scandinavians and a large dog.

A: *A happy medium.*
Q: What do you get if you tell jokes at a seance?

A: *Ran out of time.*
Q: What did the Hickory Dickory mouse do at 1 o'clock?

A: *A hardened criminal.*
Q: If a thief falls into cement, what does he become?

A: *Nitty-gritty.*
Q: What kind of wool do you get from muddy sheep?

A: *Cool, calm and collected.*
Q: How does your stamp album feel when it's kept in the refrigerator?

A: *Uncanny.*

Q: How did Mother Hubbard describe her cupboard when she found it empty?

A: *Dog-eat-dog.*

Q: If Mother Hubbard found a frankfurter for her dog, what kind of world would it be?

A: *Tom Sawyer.*

Q: How did Tom know you swiped the cookies?

A: *A hammock.*

Q: What's a sailor's knapsack (nap sack) called?

A: *In a class by himself.*

Q: How do you describe a boy who goes to school on a holiday?

A: *Tycoon.*

Q: What do you call a raccoon that wears bow ties?

· 4 ·
CHEWY
RIDDLES

On the next page you'll find some riddle puzzles for your brain to chew on! Try to figure them out before you turn the page to check the answers.

1)   Fill me up, heat me up, I won't shirk.
     In fact, I'll whistle while I work.

2)   What is this:

LB LB LB LB LB
WEIGHT

3)   I stand like a sailor with two legs spread.
     I have a belt and a pointed head.
     What letter am I?

4)   Riddle me round-about, what am I?
     Shaped like an egg, sometimes a pie.
     I've a short tail and you'll notice, too,
     I'm always followed around by "you."

5)   I'm a capital, upright fellow.
     My arms reach toward the skies.
     I stand with 25 comrades
     Right before your "eyes."

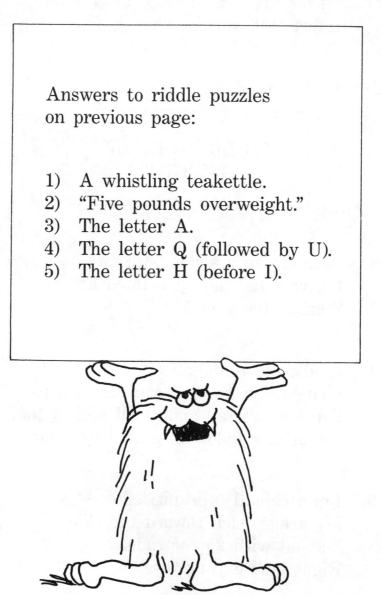

Answers to riddle puzzles
on previous page:

1) A whistling teakettle.
2) "Five pounds overweight."
3) The letter A.
4) The letter Q (followed by U).
5) The letter H (before I).

6) According to an old proverb, which of these is better:

   or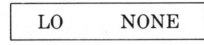

7) According to another proverb, which of these is better?

LO   NONE

8) I'm a roof, a red roof,
   Yet have no house below.
   Every time you chew your food
   Up and down I go.

9) Mark my words and mark them well,
   I've a very fine name to tell.
   You've heard it twice, but in this rhyme
   I shall tell you one more time.
   Pick up your pencil, do not frown,
   And on your paper mark it down.

10) A fuzzy face, but she never shaves.
    Name her Melba, everyone raves.

Answers to riddle puzzles
on previous page:

6) The first because "Two heads are better than one."
7) The first because "Half a loaf is better than none."
8) The roof of your mouth.
9) The name is Mark.
10) A peach.

11) Mr. and Mrs. Tyme hoped their baby would be born before midnight of December 31 so that they could take a tax deduction that year. The baby arrived at 11:59 p.m. What did the Tymes name him?

12) Astronaut, cosmonaut share my name
And nautical sailors tell you the same.
Put in a necktie, I'm not out of place,
But shoes are a mess when I'm found
    in a lace.
What am I?

13) What is this:

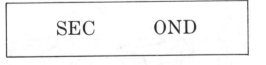

14) Babbles at stones, spits at fires,
Runs all day but never tires.
Sometimes falls, but never stumbles,
Sometimes spouts, but never grumbles.

15) Not a donkey, not a mule,
No, I'm a kind of mare.
If I appear when you're asleep
You're sure to get a scare!

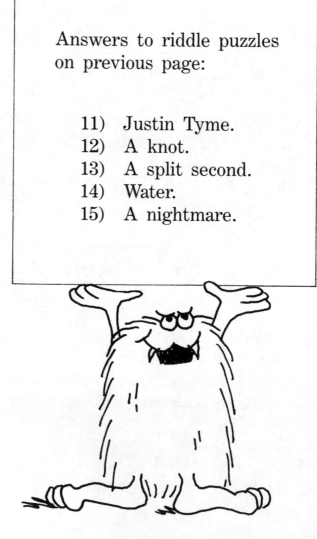

Answers to riddle puzzles
on previous page:

11)   Justin Tyme.
12)   A knot.
13)   A split second.
14)   Water.
15)   A nightmare.

16) What does this say:

YOU   JUST   ME

17) Are any of these words MISSPELLED?
   a. cawtion
   b. beeware
   c. trick
   d. quesstion

18) What is this:

P O

(HINT: *It's something you play.*)

19) Take ⅖ of a bison, ⅓ of an elk, and the
   last quarter of a mule,
   And you'll have something handy for
   riding to school.

20) I'm not sweet, yet I'm a kind of jam,
   I'm not sticky, yet you get stuck in me.
   What am I?

Answers to riddle puzzles on previous page:

16) "Just between you and me."

17) No, none of those words is the word MISSPELLED, although CAUTION, BEWARE and QUESTION are spelled wrong. (Did you notice the warning that this was a trick question?)

18) Piano (P an' O). Or you could have guessed "Post Office," also an acceptable answer.

19) Bike (bi plus k plus e).

20) A traffic jam.

• 5 •
PET TALK

Which dogs bark more, old ones or young ones?

About arf and arf (half and half).

Why does a mouse like the letter S?

It makes the cat scat!

What goes "Zzzzz, meow, zzzzz, meow"?

Someone taking a cat nap.

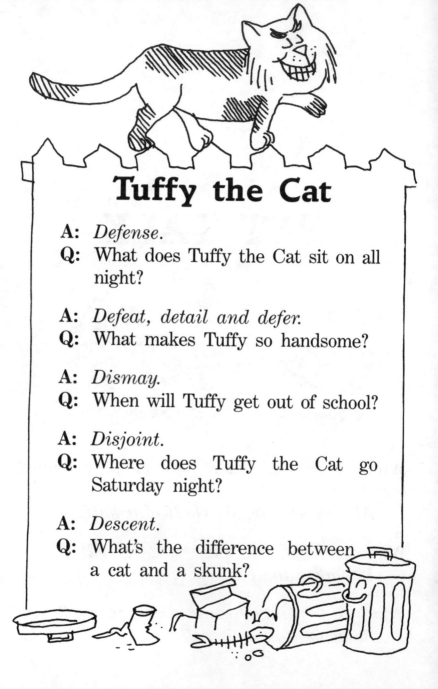

Tuffy the Cat

A: *Defense.*
Q: What does Tuffy the Cat sit on all night?

A: *Defeat, detail and defer.*
Q: What makes Tuffy so handsome?

A: *Dismay.*
Q: When will Tuffy get out of school?

A: *Disjoint.*
Q: Where does Tuffy the Cat go Saturday night?

A: *Descent.*
Q: What's the difference between a cat and a skunk?

When does a cat like a cat nap?
After a nip at the catnip.

What should you feed an overweight cat?
Slender (Tender) Vittles.

What animals do scouts take on overnight trips?
Pup tents and first-aid kits.

What part of a tent is hardest to keep clean?
The ground floor.

How did pioneer puppies go west?
In waggin' (wagon) trains.

How can a dog get rid of ticks?
By taking off its wrist watch.

Why do dogs run in circles?
It's hard to run in squares.

What two things can a circle do that a square can't?
Stand 'round and be nothing.

Why didn't the church mouse live in the steeple?
She didn't a-spire that high.

The Joint Is Jumping

What has big eyes, green skin, and lives alone?
Hermit the Frog.

How does a frog cross a busy street?
He hops a bus.

Why don't frogs make good workers?
They're too hoppy-go-lucky.

When does a tadpole wear little pink satin shoes?
For her toad-dancing lesson.

What should you say when you meet a toad?
"Wart's new?"

Why did the cat hang around the stereo?
*He hoped to catch the tweeter for lunch—
if the woofer didn't get him first!*

Why did the rich woman put on the dog?
Her jacket was at the cleaners.

What do you get if you cross bubble gum, a hen, and a dog?
Snap, cackle and pup.

What do you get if you cross a turtle and a boomerang?
Snappy comebacks.

What do you get if you cross a hen and a parrot?
A bird that uses really fowl (foul) language.

6 •
SUPERSTARS & OTHER GREATS

Why did all the king's men laugh at Humpty Dumpty?
They thought he was a big yolk (joke).

What do you call a sheep that hangs out with 40 thieves?
Ali Baa Baa.

What do you call an elephant that hangs out with 40 thieves?
Ali Babar.

Does Bo Peep have fleas?
No, all her fleas are on the lam (lamb).

Why do the police keep tabs on Bo Peep?
Because she goes around with a crook.

Who was unhappy at the way his suit came back from the cleaners?
Ripped van Wrinkled (Rip van Winkle).

Can you name someone who's a good boxer?
Sure—it's right up Muhammad's alley (Ali).

What's made of chicken and rice and is faster than a speeding bullet?
Chicken Soup-erman.

What was Chicken Souperman's other name?
Cluck Kent.

What turkey starred in *Gone with the Wind*?
Clark Gobble (Gable).

Who writes mystery stories and blooms in spring?
Edgar Allan Poe-sy.

Will Mrs. Alcott ever write a book called *Little Women*?
No, but Louisa May.

Why did the famous spy, Mata Hari, always look sad?

She was no laughing Mata.

Why didn't Queen Elizabeth I ever marry?

No suitor could suit 'er.

What Scottish king was round and had a hole in the middle?

King Duncan Doughnut.

Who sings in English but is located in South America?

Bolivia Newton-John.

Moo-ving Right Along

Why did Elsie the Cow go to Hollywood?

To be a moo-vie star.

Did Elsie the Cow get to be a movie star?

No, but she made lots of moo-lah.

What kind of car did Elsie the Cow drive?

A moo-ving van.

How is a kid tossing a ball like a cow?

A kid tossing a ball is a pitcher; a pitcher is a milk container; and a milk container is a cow!

What flies, does magic, and has no name?
An Unidentified Flying Sorcerer.

What would you call an expert in mud wrestling?
The Wizard of Ooze.

How do we know Jack and Jill were royalty?
Because when Jack fell down he broke his crown.

Who has six legs, wears a coonskin cap, and chirps?
Davy Cricket (Crockett).

Who invents telephones and carries your luggage?
Alexander Graham Bellhop.

What has a curly tail and a snout, and wears a red, white and blue costume?
Oinkle (Uncle) Sam.

What has curly hair and says "Arf, Arf"?
Little Arfin' (Orphan) Annie.

What dog gets rusty if you leave him out in the rain?
Rin Tin Tin.

What's the difference between St. George and Rudolf the Red-nosed Reindeer?

One slays the dragon and the other's draggin' the sleigh.

Where does Santa stay overnight when he travels?

At ho-ho-hotels.

Why doesn't Santa live at the South Pole?

His reindeer don't like to eat upside down.

• 7 •
MR. PRESIDENT, MR. PRESIDENT!

Which president had big sharp teeth?
Jaws (George) Washington.

Which president was solid wood and had roomy drawers?
Martin Van Bureau (Van Buren).

Which one was good at starting fires?
William McKindling (McKinley).

Which president was a great help to Santa?
Chimney (Jimmy) Carter.

Which president made a nice pie for Washington's birthday?
Cherry (Gerry) Ford.

Which president kept Washington, D.C. in stitches?
Zachary Tailor (Taylor).

Which one liked horror films?
Calvin Ghoulidge (Coolidge).

Which president reminds you of a doorbell?
Chimes (James) Madison.

Which president liked to dance?
James Knox Polka (Polk).

Which one liked daffy jokes?
William Howard Daft (Taft).

Which one acted like a clown?
Jester (Chester) A. Arthur.

Which president was a dentist in his spare time?
Millard Fillmore.

Which one never had to wear a wig?
Hairy (Harry) Truman.

Which had trouble with the dogcatcher?
Rover (Grover) Cleveland.

Which president was orange-flavored?
Sherbet (Herbert) Hoover.

Which president talked like a pig?
Ulysses S. Grunt (Grant).

• 8 •
LOVE & HISSES

What happens when you fall in love with a gambler?

He cheats on you.

What happens when you fall in love with a telephone operator?

She gives you a phone-y line.

What happens when you fall in love with a trashman?

He dumps you.

What happens when you fall in love with a clockmaker?
She two-times you.

What happens when you fall in love with a pastry cook?
He desserts (deserts) you.

What happens when you fall in love with a shoe salesman?
He walks all over you.

What happens when you fall in love with an elevator?
It lets you down.

They're Playing Our Song

What's a doe's favorite song?
   "I Only Have Eyes for You, Deer."

What's a ram's favorite?
   "I Only Have Eyes for Ewe, Dear."

What's the iceman's favorite?
   "I Only Have Ice for You, Dear."

How does a spelling champ sing it?
   "I Only Have I's for U, Dear."

They're Playing Our Song

How does a cowboy sing it?
"I Own Levi's for You, Dear."

How does a bored person sing it?
"I Yawnly Have Eyes for You, Dear."

How does an old sailor sing it?
"I Only Have Aye-Ayes for You, Sir."

What happens when you fall in love with an artist?

You get the brush.

What happens when you fall in love with a trench digger?

You get ditched.

What happens when you fall in love with a jogger?

You get the run-around.

What happens when you fall in love with an underwear salesman?

You get the slip.

What happens when you fall in love with a chauffeur?

You get taken for a ride.

What happens when you fall in love with a French chef?

You get buttered up.

· 9 ·
REVERSE
RIDDLES

A: *Doe-si-doe.*

Q: What happens when two deer meet at a square dance?

A: *Hoedown.*

Q: What's a farmer's favorite dance?

A: *Despair.*
Q: What comes in handy when you have a flat tire?

A: *Tom Thumb.*
Q: What does Tom do when his car breaks down?

A: *Eavesdropping.*
Q: What's a sign that your roof needs repair?

A: *Silver polish.*
Q: How does the Lone Ranger keep his horse so shiny?

A: *Bassinet.*

Q: What makes a fisherman happy?

A: *Wishy-washy.*

Q: What do you call washday at your fairy godmother's house?

A: *Flying saucers.*

Q: What do flying cups land on?

A: *Mississippi.*

Q: Who's married to Mr. Sippi?

A: *Yard work.*
Q: If you had three feet, what kind of work would you do?

A: *Undersecretary of State.*
Q: Where is the Secretary of State's chair?

A: *Pigeon-toed.*
Q: Who squealed on the cat?

A: *A pair of drawers.*
Q: Who were Picasso and Michelangelo?

A: *Chairman of the Board.*

Q: Who yawns the most?

A: *Afterward.*

Q: Where does "ware" appear in the dictionary?

A: *An outstanding pupil.*

Q: If the teacher makes you stand outside, what are you?

A: *Home Sweet Home.*

Q: What did Hansel and Gretel call the gingerbread house?

A: *It was just a harebrained idea.*

Q: Why did the rabbit start hiding Easter eggs?

A: *Blackmail.*

Q: If your letter carrier falls in the mud, what do you get?

A: *Stupidity and calamity.*
Q: What kinds of tea are best to avoid?

A: *Goldie Hawn.*
Q: What do you find in a brass band?

A: *Chrysanthemum.*
Q: What flower was named after Christopher Columbus and his mother?

A: *Mohair.*
Q: What does a balding man want?

A: *Goblet.*
Q: What will a dog do to steak?

A: *Bumpkin.*
Q: What kind of pies do hillbillies eat at Thanksgiving?

A: *Hiccups.*
Q: What do hillbillies drink from?

A: *Medium rare.*
Q: What is an unusual fortune-teller called?

A: *Shady deals.*
Q: What do cardplayers get under a chestnut tree?

• 10 •
ANIMAL
FARE

What does a parrot say on the Fourth of July?

"Polly want a firecracker!"

What would you call a bird that joins the Ice Capades?

A cheep skate.

Where do woodpeckers conduct their business?

In branch offices.

How do you drive a centipede crazy?

Ask him to put his best foot forward.

It's Gnus (News) to Me

How do we know gnus are smarter than dogs?

Because you can't teach an old dog gnu tricks.

Why did the little gnu stay home from school?

She had gnu-monia (pneumonia).

Why were Santa's reindeer worried?

Santa said he might get a gnu sleigh.

Are there gnus in Europe?

Yes, we hear foreign gnus on TV every day.

It's Gnus (News) to Me

Is it true that gnus are fussy housekeepers?

Yes, a gnu broom sweeps clean!

Do gnus work on farms?

Yes, most farms have fields of gnu-mown hay.

Do gnus like delicatessen food?

Yes, there's a Gnu Deli (New Delhi) in India.

Why should you avoid shaking hands with a gnu?

There's a lot of shocking gnus around these days.

Where do sea gulls (girls) like to hang out?
Where the buoys (boys) are.

Why did the canary lose its voice?
It didn't have enough tweet (to eat).

Why do bees fly?
They're too buzzy (busy) to wait for a bus.

How do you make a pig fly?
Add e-o-n to its name and it turns into a pigeon.

Why do kangaroos make good football players?
They're never out of bounds.

What do kangaroos read?
Pocketbooks.

Where do little bears sit on a train?
In the cub-oose (caboose).

Moo-ving Right Along

What do you get if you cross a cow with a belly dancer?
Milkshakes.

What do you get from a cow that reads *Reader's Digest?*
Condensed milk.

What do you get from a forgetful cow?
Milk of Amnesia.

What do you get from an invisible cow?
Evaporated milk.

What do you get from a magician's cow?
Vanishing cream.

Moo-ving Right Along

What do you get from an Alaskan cow?

Cold cream.

What do you get from a funny cow?
Cream of wit.

What do you get from a cow that tells bad jokes?
Creamed corn.

Why don't cows like to tell jokes?
Because they're often in a bad moo-ed.

Do cows often graze alone?
Herdly ever.

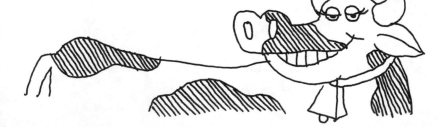

What did the walrus say to the polar bear?
"Have an ice (a nice) day!"

What did the horses say at the Town Meeting?
They voted neigh (nay).

What is grey, has large ears, and goes squeak, squeak?
An elephant wearing new shoes.

When does an elephant use Ivory Soap?
When he washes his tusks.

What do you get if you cross an elephant with a Model T car?

Either a cranky elephant or a car with a very large trunk.

What do you get if you cross a laughing hyena and an elephant?

Dr. Chuckle and Mr. Hide.

What do you get if you cross a Boy Scout and a giraffe?

A boy everyone looks up to.

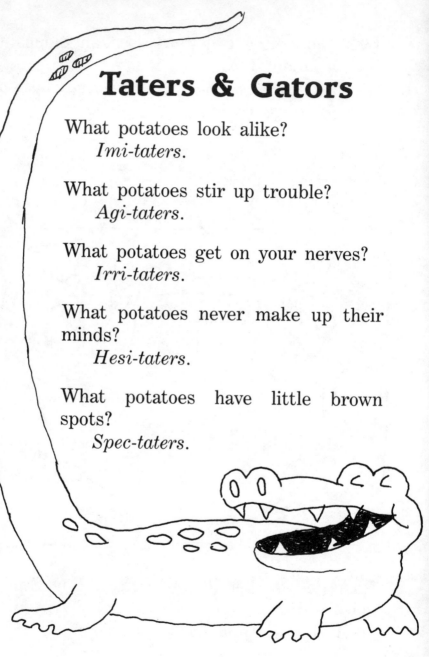

Taters & Gators

What potatoes look alike?
Imi-taters.

What potatoes stir up trouble?
Agi-taters.

What potatoes get on your nerves?
Irri-taters.

What potatoes never make up their minds?
Hesi-taters.

What potatoes have little brown spots?
Spec-taters.

Taters & Gators

What alligators love cream cheese on a bagel?
Dele-gators (deli-gators).

What alligators go to church socials?
Congre-gators.

What alligators join the Navy?
Navi-gators.

What alligators join the FBI?
Investi-gators.

What alligators prefer old-fashioned phones?
Croco-dials.

How come animals can't keep secrets?
Because pigs squeal, yaks yak, and someone always lets the cat out of the bag.

Why do lions roar?
They would feel silly saying "Oink, oink."

How come fish get so much mail?
Someone is always dropping them a line.

What's the easiest way to fill a pen?
Round up a bunch of pigs and push them inside.

It's Gnus (News) to Me

Where do gnus live?
In Gnu Hampshire, Gnu Jersey, Gnu Mexico, Gnu York, and there are also some in Gnu Brunswick and Gnufoundland.

Are gnus full of mischief?
Yes, no gnus is good gnus.

Why should you invite a toad and a gnu to your New Year's Eve party?
So you'll have a Hoppy Gnu Year!

Why does an octopus need lots of phones?
So it can reach out and touch someone.

What do you get if you cross an octopus with a clock?
Either a clock with 8 hands or an octopus that's really ticked off.

What would you do if Moby Dick swallowed you?
Whale (wail)!

· 11 ·
FAMILY TIES

If your brother had a split personality, who would he be?
Your half brother.

If your mother was very tiny, what would you call her?
Minimum.

If your mother sang like a little bird, what would you call her?
Malarkey.

Anti-Auntie

If your aunt had a big appetite, what would she be?
An anteater.

If she had an upset stomach, what would you call her?
Antacid.

If she was always cold, what would you call her?
Anti-freeze.

If your aunt was very fond of you, what would she be?
Antidote.

If she thought she was an airplane, what would you call her?
Anti-aircraft.

If she forgot to get off the bus at O Street, what would she be?
Antipasto.

Anti-Auntie

If your aunt had rabbit ears, what would she be?
>*Antenna.*

If she ran off to get married, what would you call her?
>*Antelope.*

If she married Mr. Hill, what would she become?
>*Ant Hill.*

If your uncle was 12 inches shorter than your aunt, what would she be?
>*Tolerant (taller aunt).*

If your aunt was very old, what would you call her?
>*Antique.*

If your mother stuck a feather in her cap, what would you call her?

Macaroni.

If she came from the Russian plains, what would she be?

Your step (steppe) mother.

If your father loved pizza with extra cheese, what would you call him?

Parcheesi.

If your father was a barber, what would you call him?

Parsnips.

If your father owned a newspaper stand, what would you call him?

Parcel Post.

If your father told dumb jokes, what would you call him?

Pop Corn.

If your father was Stephen Foster, what would that make you?

A Foster child.

• 12 •
RHYME TIME

What kind of spook always gives you an argument?

A squabblin' goblin.

What spook throws the best party?

A ghost host.

What kind of joke makes a violin laugh?

A fiddle riddle.

What do some folks get when they're 65 years old?
A desire to retire.

When Rip Van Winkle woke up after 20 years, what did he have on his face?
A weird beard.

What noise do sleeping lions make?
Roaring snoring!

What do you get when you tell geese too many riddles?
Bonkers honkers!

What does a jellyfish see when it looks in the mirror?
A squishy fishy.

What bear likes ginger ale?
A fizzly grizzly.

What does your dog give you that no one else can?
A pooch smooch.

What do you call a bunch of dopey cows?
A nerd herd.

What do you get if you don't give your taxi driver a tip?
A crabby cabby.

What kind of nose does a fat pig have?
A stout snout.

What did Miss Piggy wear on her head when she went to the party?
A piglet wiglet.

• 13 •
SILLY
GILLY

What happened when Silly Gilly left her library book outdoors?

In the morning it was over dew (overdue).

Why did Silly Gilly pour alphabet soup in her pocket?

She wanted to be a letter carrier.

Why didn't Silly Gilly answer the door?

She thought it was her knees knocking.

What kind of hat did Silly Gilly wear to the Auto Show?

A hub cap.

When Silly Gilly bought panty hose that had a snag, what did she get?

A run for her money.

Why did Silly Gilly put a clock under her desk?

The boss asked her to work overtime.

Why did Silly Gilly tell everyone she was engaged?

Because her boyfriend said he'd give her a ring one night.

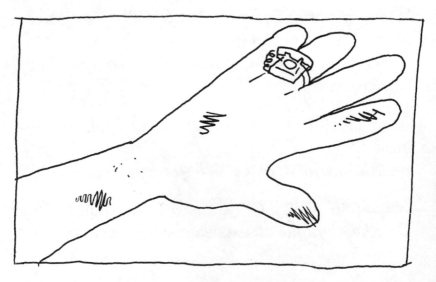

Why did Silly Gilly's boyfriend keep a stiff upper lip?
Someone starched his moustache.

If a lifeguard wanted to marry Silly Gilly, what would he be?
Her bathing suit-or.

Why didn't Silly Gilly like the joke about the Grand Canyon?
It was too deep.

Why didn't she like the joke about the shellac?
It was pretty tacky.

Why didn't she like the ocean joke?
She couldn't fathom it.

Did Silly Gilly believe the story about the sleeping soldier?
No, it was a lot of bunk.

Did she believe the story about the sword?
No, she couldn't swallow it.

Did she believe the story about the sandwich?
No, it was full of baloney (bologna).

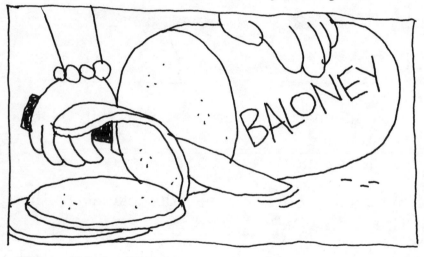

Why didn't Silly Gilly finish the book about the palace kidnapping?
Too many pages were missing.

Did Silly Gilly like the story about the bath towel?
It was very absorbing.

How about the story about the snake trainers?
It was rather charming.

Did she like the story about the dog who chased the stick for two miles?
No, it was too far-fetched.

What did she say about the Venus de Milo story?
It was disarming.

Did Silly Gilly like the story about the drill?
She thought it was a bore!

Was she surprised at the story about the carpet?
Yes, it nearly floored her!

• 14 •
THE CART BEFORE THE HORSE

A: *Horse and buggy.*

Q: How do you feel when you have a sore throat and fleas?

A: *Polka.*

Q: What should you do when your sister falls asleep in church?

A: *General Hospital.*

Q: What has 3 stars, 500 bedpans, and must be saluted every day?

A: *Fish cake.*

Q: What do you bake for your guppy's birthday?

A: *The whale spout.*

Q: How do you know when whales are sulking?

A: *Polliwogs.*

Q: How does Polly get to school?

A: *"Piggyback!"*
Q: What did Fozzie say to Kermit when his girlfriend came home?

A: *A pigtail.*
Q: What is Miss Piggy's life story?

A: *Unauthorized.*
Q: What is an anonymous story?

A: *Ignoramus.*
Q: What shall we do if Amos acts silly?

A: *Grammar school.*
Q: Is your grandmother hip?

A: *Tulane University.*

Q: What college teaches you how to drive on a divided highway?

A: *Egyptian mummy.*

Q: Who is married to an Egyptian daddy?

A: *Oscar Wilde.*

Q: What was Oscar before he was tamed?

A: *Molasses.*

Q: What do you get when you cross moles and donkeys?

A: *Banana splits.*

Q: What happens when a banana hears a good joke?

A: *Pandemonium.*
Q: What does a panda do when it hears a terrible joke?

A: *Needlepoint.*
Q: What goes on inside a compass?

A: *Milk pitcher, soup dish and sugar bowl.*
Q: Name two containers and a football stadium.

A: *Out of whack.*
Q: How does a tired baseball player feel?

STRIKE THREE!

A: *Neck and neck.*

Q: What would you see through the window of a giraffe's house?

A: *Football.*

Q: What do you call it if your toes have a good cry?

A: *Incognito.*

Q: What do you call a toe that's in disguise?

A: *Bermuda shorts.*

Q: What do they call pygmies in Bermuda?

A: *Himalayan.*

Q: What's the lazy boy doing in the hammock?

A: *An orangu-tan.*

Q: What does an orangu get at the beach?

A: *Frostbite.*

Q: What must you beware of if you give a snowman false teeth?

A: *Snow Belt.*

Q: What holds up a snowman's pants?

A: *Commentator.*

Q: What do you call a plain old potato?

A: *Chopsticks.*

Q: What happens to the lamb chop if you don't grease the pan?

A: *Paramount Pictures.*

Q: What are Mt. Vesuvius and Mt. Everest, nicely framed?

A: *Semi-sweet.*

Q: Is Sammy a good little baby?

A: *Divan.*

Q: What does Prince Charles call his wife's car?

A: *Chuck wagon.*

Q: And what does Princess Di call his car?

A: *Hurdy-gurdy.*

Q: What did the hammer do when Gert hit her thumb with it?

A: *The apple core.*

Q: If a worm can't get into the Marine Corps, what can he join?

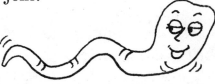

• 15 •
YOU NAME IT

What was the name of William Penn's brother?

Bic.

What was the name of Gandhi's sister?

Penny (penny candy).

Who was Peeping Tom's sister?

Little Bo Peeping.

What did the rancher name his son?
Brandon.

What was the name of the car salesman?
Otto.

If Millicent changes her name to Millie, what will happen?
She won't have a cent to her name.

What did Little Mary Sunshine name her baby?
Ray.

What did Snow White name her baby?
Egg.

What did Mrs. T. name her baby?
E.

What was the name of Cinderella's fairy godmother?
Wanda.

What did the thief name his son?
Robin.

· 16 ·
PEOPLE, PLACES
& THINGS

Is the weather good in Brazil?
  Yes, it's never Chile.

What happened when it rained on Uranus?
The Mercury fell, Pluto Saturn (sat in) a puddle, and by Jupiter, nobody ever did planet (plan it) that way!

Why is a river after a flood like a large dictionary?
It's un-abridged.

What word of three syllables is always mispronounced?
"Mispronounced."

Why is H the most popular letter?
It's the start of every holiday!

And why is O the cheeriest letter?
It's always in a good mood and never out of sorts.

What sizes do crowns come in?
King-size and queen-size.

What do you get if you cross ladies' underwear with part of your shoe?
A slip of the tongue.

Double Trouble

What do you need most when you're waiting to see the doctor?
Patient's patience.

What would you like to wipe off your eyeglasses?
Specs specks.

What do you need to make if you want to stay overnight in a teepee?
A reservation reservation.

How did the scarecrow describe its job?
Guardin' the garden.

What kind of canary does a bargain hunter look for?
A cheaper cheeper.

Double Trouble

What beast can't tell the truth?
A lyin' lion.

What do you have if your foot is 12 inches long?
A foot foot.

What did the father of 10 girls say when another baby girl arrived?
Alas—a lass!

What does Count Dracula have at the bank?
A Count account.

When is a light bulb like a curious kid?
When it's 100 whats (watts).

How is a robbery different from a spoiled girl?
One is a stick-up and the other is stuck-up.

What is the best thing to do before you take a bath?
Undress.

What goes over your head and under your feet but doesn't cover your body?
A jump rope.

When is a foot not a foot?
When it's ahead in a race. And that's quite a feat!

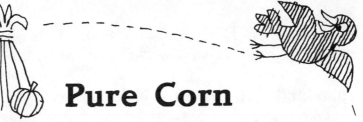

Pure Corn

In what bed is it perfectly okay to dump manure?

A flower bed.

Why did the petunias want to move?

They grew up in a seedy neighborhood.

What goes in one ear and out the other?

A bug in a cornfield.

What do you get if a little bear sits in the cornfield?

Corn on the cub.

What does an Eskimo put on his bed?
A sheet of ice and a blanket of snow.

What kind of lettuce do Eskimos eat?
Iceberg.

Where did the Old Lady Who Lived in a Shoe send her kids in the summer?
To boot camp.

What can you pay your teacher, even if you haven't a cent?
Attention.

Why is it dangerous to yawn at the beach?
You might get tongue tide (tied).

What color is popular at football games?
Yell-ow.

Why is it so noisy in the forest?
The dogwood barks and the willow is weeping.

Why do people say you saw wood when you snore?
Maybe because there's lumber in slumber.

What happens to cigars after dinner?
They meet their match.

Why are A and E the craziest vowels?
They're both in sane.

Why did the piggy bank yell "Ouch!"?
Because the miser pinched his pennies.

Why is T a generous letter?
Without it every mister would be a miser.

What's the difference between a new suit and a fireplace grate?
The suit looks great but the grate looks sooty.

What did the broom say to the vacuum cleaner?
"Don't you wish people would stop pushing us around?"

What happens when you don't dust your mirror?
It gives you a dirty look.

• 17 •
STUMPERS

Here are some real toughies to try on the sharpest riddlers you know:

Why didn't Eve have any sisters?
  Because Adam had no spare ribs.

What do you find at supper in a Paris monastery?
  An order of French friars (fries).

What do you get if you cross the Tower of Pisa and Miss Piggy?

Lean pork chops.

Why was the gardener so happy when he crossed a fruit and a vegetable?

He got a raisin celery (a raise in salary).

What did the tailor get when he crossed a fireplace with a vegetable?

A three-peas soot (3-piece suit).

If a tailor is in an empty room with nothing but a fireplace, how does he get his ironing done?

He just picks up the fireplace andirons (and irons).

What do you get if you cross a Boy Scout and the Hoover Dam?

Knot by a dam site.

What do you get if you cross berries and a grand piano?

Raspberry Schubert (sherbet).

What composer keeps the neighbors awake with his woof-ing?

Johann Sebastian Bark (Bach).

Why is it so noisy in a library?

Because Mike Hammers, Ezra Pounds and, during the Christmas season, Lewis Carrolls.

What musical instrument does a frog play?

The hopsichord (harpsichord).

How was Shakespeare different from "The Man Without a Country"?

One was a bard from England and the other was barred from America.

How is a pushy person like your porch in winter?

They both get icy stares (stairs).

What bird was first to fly over the North Pole?
Admiral Richard Byrd.

What's soft, eggy, and took a stand at Little Big Horn?
General Custard (Custer).

What famous remark did Mo's wife make when he went shopping?
"Remember the alum, Mo (Alamo)!"

What did the waitress say to the chef?
"Give me a little quiche (kiss)!"

What has big eyes, green skin and writes silly verses?
Frogden (Ogden) Nash.

What's 5,600 feet tall and has four heads?
Mt. Rushmore.

What would you say if you were to meet the Dog Star in person?
"You can't be Sirius (serious)!"

What's the difference between a man with a missing slipper and a detective trailing a criminal?
One suspects his dog and the other dogs his suspect.

How is a large apartment like a candy store?
One is a suite of rooms; the other is a room of sweets.

What do you get if you cross a doorbell and a doughnut?

Ring around the cruller.

Why did the little ghost's lemon meringue pie fly back and hit her?

It was a boo-meringue (boomerang) pie.

Where do Russian spooks live?

In Outer Mon-ghoulia (Mongolia).

What do you say to a skeleton crew when it goes sailing?

"Bone (bon) voyage!"

INDEX

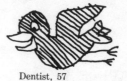

Actor, 22, 23
Adam and Eve, 119
Agent, secret, 13
Airplane, 86
Alamo, 123
Alaska, 77
Alcott, Louisa May, 49
Ali Baba, 47
Alligator, 28, 81
Alphabet soup, 93
Ankles, 26
Ant hill, 87
Anteater, 86
Antelope, 87
Apartment, 124
Appetite, 86
Army, 9; officers, 15
Arthur, Chester, 57
Artist, 22, 62
Astrologer, 11
Auntie, 86-87

Baby, naming the, 108
Bach, J.S., 122
Balding man, 69
Ball, 51
Banana, 101
Bank, 113
Barber, 89
Baseball, 22, 102
Basketball player, 21
Bath, 114; towel, 96
Bats, 7
Beach, 104, 116
Beard, 91
Bears, 75, 78, 92, 115
Bed, 115
Bees, 74
Bell, Alexander Graham,
  53
Bellhop, 8
Belly: button, 26; dancer,
  76
Bermuda, 103
Berries, 121
Bike, 39, 40
Bikini, 5
Bird, 71, 123
Birthday, 99
Blackmail, 68
Bluejay, 8
Bo Peep, 48, 106
Boa constrictors, 17
Bolivia, 50
Book, 93
Boomerang, 46
Boxer, 48

Boy scout, 79, 121
Brazil, 109
Breakfast, 11, 27
Broom, 118
Brother, 85
Bubble gum, 46
Bucharest, 10
Budapest, 10
Bus, 86

Calendar, 14
Canary, 74, 112
Candy store, 124
Cannibal, 10
Car, 51, 79, 105;
  salesman, 107
Carpenter, 16
Carpet, 97
Carroll, Lewis, 122
Carter, Jimmy, 56
Cathedral, 15
Cats, 41-43, 46, 66, 82
Centipede, 71
Chairman of the Board,
  67
Charles, Prince, 105
Chauffeur, 62
Chefs, 12, 62, 123
Chicken, 49
Chopsticks, 105
Christmas, 122
Chrysanthemum, 69
Church, 44, 81, 98
Cigars, 117
Cinderella, 108
Circus, 23
Cleaners, 48
Cleveland, Grover, 57
Clock, 84, 94; maker, 59
Clown, 57
Coffee, 11, 13
Color, 117
Columbus, Christopher,
  69
Compass, 102
Composer, 122
Coolidge, Calvin, 56
Corn, 115
Cowboy, 61
Cows, 51, 76-77, 92
Critics, 23
Crockett, Davy, 52
Crowns, 111

Dance, 57, 63
Deer, 63
Delicatessens, 73, 81
Demons, 7

Dentist, 57
Desserts, 59
Detective, 124
Di, Princess, 105
Dictionary, 110
Doctor, 112
Doe, 60
Dog, 41, 43, 44, 46, 53,
  70, 72, 92, 97, 124;
  catcher, 57
Donut, 50
Doorbell, 57, 125
Double Trouble, 112-113
Doughnut, 125
Dr. Pepper, 28
Dracula, 11, 113
Dragon, 54
Dressmakers, 20
Drill, 97
Duncan, King, 50

Easter eggs, 68
Elephants, 5, 47, 78, 79
Elevator, 59
Elizabeth I, 50
Elsie the Cow, 51
Eskimos, 116
E.T., 27, 108
Eyeglasses, 112

Fairy godmother, 65
Families, 85-89
Farmers, 18-19, 63
Farms, 73
Father, 89, 113
FBI, 81
Fillmore, Millard, 57
Fires, 56
Fish, 82, 92, 99
Fisherman, 65
Flat tire, 64
Fleas, 48, 98
Flying saucers, 65
Food, 11
Foot, 113, 114
Football, 103, 117;
  players, 75; stadium,
  102
Ford, Gerry, 56
Forebears, 27
Forest, 117
Foster, Stephen, 89
Fozzie bear, 27, 100
French chef, 62
Frogs, 8, 9, 45, 122, 123

Gable, Clark, 49
Gambler, 58

Gandhi, 106
Gardner, 120
Garter, 20
Gators, 81
Geese, 91
Ghosts, 6, 7, 12, 90, 125
Ghoul, 12
Giant, 12
Gingerbread house, 67
Giraffe, 79, 103
Gnus, 72-73, 83
Goblin, 90
Gone with the Wind, 49
Goose, 19, 29
Grand Canyon, 95
Grandmother, 100
Grant, Ulysses S., 57
Grapes, 18

Hair, 12
Hammer, Mike, 122
Hammock, 31, 104
Handshaking, 73
Hansel and Gretel, 67
Hat, 94
Hawn, Goldie, 69
Heads, 35, 36
Heaven, 10
Hen, 46; house, 19
Hiccups, 70
Hickory Dickory mouse, 30
Hillbillies, 70
Holiday, 31
Hollywood, 51
Hoover: Dam, 121; Herbert, 57
Horror films, 56
Horse, 19, 78; and buggy, 98
Hospital, 10
Housekeepers, 73
Hubbard, Mother, 31
Humpty Dumpty, 47
Hurdy-gurdy, 105
Hyena, laughing, 79

Ice Capades, 71
Iceman, 60
India, 73
Intuition, 63
"I Only Have Eyes for You," 60-61
Ivory soap, 78

Jack and Jill, 52
Jam, 10
Jelly, 10 fish, 92
Jobs, 13-24
Jogger, 62
Joint Is Jumping, 8-9, 45

Jokes, 29, 47, 57, 77, 89, 90, 95, 101, 102
Judge, 14
July 4th, 71
Jump rope, 114
Jury, 14
Justin Tyme, 37, 38

Kangaroos, 75
Kermit, 100
King Kong, 24
Knot, 37, 38

Lamb, 48
Lawyer, 13
Letters, 111, 118
Lettuce, 116
Library, 122
Lifeguard, 95
Light bulb, 114
Lions, 82, 91, 113
Lip, stiff upper, 95
Little Big Horn, 123
Little Mary Sunshine, 108
Little Orphan Annie, 53
Little Women, 49
Loaf, half a, 35, 36
Locksmith, 14
Lone Ranger, 64
Love, falling in, 58-62
Lumberjack, 24
Lunch, 12

Macaroni, 88
Madison, James, 57
Magician, 23
Manure, 115
"Man Without a Country," 122
Marine Corps, 105
Marionette, 27
Mark, 35, 36
Mata Hari, 50
McDonald's, 27
McKinley, William, 56
Mealtime, 19
Medium, 10, 29, 70
Melba, 35, 36
Mermaid, 11
Mice, 22
Michelangelo, 66
Milk, 51, 76
Mirror, 92, 118
Mischief, 83
Miser, 118
Miss Piggy, 23, 100, 120
Missionary, 10
Mississippi, 65
Misspellings, 39, 40
Moby Dick, 84
Model T, 79

Molasses, 101
Moo-ving Right Along, 51
Mother, 85, 88; Hubbard, 31; Whistler's, 24
Mount Vernon, 25
Mountains, 105
Mouse, 41, 44
Moustache, 95
Mouth, roof of, 35, 36
Movies, 24
Movie star, 51
Mud wrestling, 52
Muhammad Ali, 48
Mummy, 101
Music, 21
Musical instrument, 122
Musician, 21

Names, 106-108
Nash, Ogden, 123
Navy, 9, 81
Needle, 20; workers, 20
New Year's Eve, 83
Newspaper stand, 89
Newton-John, Olivia, 50
Nightmare, 37, 38
North Pole, 123
Nose drops, 26

Ocean, 95
Octopus, 84
Orangutan, 104
Overboard, man, 14
Overshoes, 26

Paddington, 27
Palace, 96
Panda, 102
Panty hose, 94
Parade, 12
Parrot, 46, 71
Party, 90, 92
Pastry cook, 59
Peeping Tom, 106
Pen, 82
Penn, William, 106
Pepper, Dr., 28
Pets, 41-46
Phones, 81, 84
Piano, 21, 39, 40, 121
Picasso, 66
Pie, 56, 70
Pig, 57, 74, 82, 92
Pigeon, 74
Piggy: bank, 118; Miss, 23, 100, 120
Pilots, 15
Pioneers, 44
Pirate, 18
Pitcher, 51
Pizza, 89

Planets, 110
Poe, Edgar Allan, 49
Polar bear, 78
Police, 48
Polk, James Knox, 57
Polliwogs, 99
Pony, 7
Post office, 39, 40
Potatoes, 80, 104
Pound, Ezra, 122
Presidents, 55-57
Prize: booby, 12; fighter, 17
Proverb, 35
Pupil, 67
Pups, 43, 44
Pure Corn, 18-19, 115
Puzzles, riddle, 32-40
Pygmies, 103

Rabbit, 68
Raccoon, 31
Radish, 27
Ram, 60
Rancher, 107
Reader's Digest, 76
Reindeer, 54, 72
Reservation, 112
Rhyming riddles, 90-92
Riddle, 90, 91
Rin Tin Tin, 53
Ring, 94
Rip van Winkle, 48, 91
River, 110
Robbery, 114
Robin, 108
Roof, 64
Rudolf the Red-Nosed Reindeer, 54
Rushmore, Mt., 124
Russian plains, 88

Safecracker, 14
Sahara Desert, 27
Sailors, 15, 31, 33, 61
Salesmen, 17, 59, 62
Sandwich, 28, 96
Santa Claus, 54, 56, 72
Sawyer, Tom, 31
Scandinavians, 29
Scarecrow, 112
School, 31
Scouts, 43
Scrooge, 11
Sea gulls, 74
Second, split, 37, 38
Secrets, 82
Seven-Up, 25
Sewing, 20
Shakespeare, William, 122

Sheep, 12, 19, 30, 47
Sheik, 28
Siberian husky, 29
Silly Gilly, 93-97
Sirius, 124
Skateboard, 19
Skating, 71
Skeleton, 7; crew, 125
Skunk, 42
Smokey, 24, 27
Snake trainers, 97
Snoring, 117
Snow White, 25, 108
Snowman, 104
Solar house, 16
Soldier, 15
Songs, favorite, 60-61
South America, 50
Spelling champ, 60
Split personality, 85
Spooks, Russian, 125
Spoons, 24
Spy, 13, 50
Square, 44; dance, 98
Stamp album, 30
St. George, 54
Stereo, 46
Stocking, 20
Stomach, upset, 86
Suit, 118
Summer camp, 116
Superman, 49
Supper, 119
Sword, 96

Tadpole, 45
Taft, William Howard, 57
Tailor, 120, 121
Taters, 80
Taxi driver, 92
Taylor, Zachary, 56
Tea, 69; kettle, 33, 34
Teacher, 21, 67
Teddy bear, 27
Teepee, 112
Teeth, brushing, 21
Telephone, 53; operator, 58
Termites, 22
Tent, 43
Thanksgiving, 70
Theatre, 22
"They're Playing Our Song," 60-61

Thief, 30, 47, 108
Throat, sore, 98
Time, 16
Tire, flat, 64
Toad, 83
Toe, 103
Tom Thumb, 64
Towel, 96
Tower of Pisa, 120
Town meeting, 78
Traffic jam, 39, 40
Train, 75; conductor, 16
Trashman, 58
Tree, 24
Trench digger, 62
Truman, Harry S., 57
Tuffy the Cat, 42
Tulane University, 101
Tulips, 26
Turkey, 49
Turtle, 46
Tycoon, 31

Uncle, 87; Sam, 53
Undersecretary of State, 66
Underwear, 111
Unidentified flying sorcerer, 52
Uranus, 110

Vacuum cleaner, 118
Vampire, 10, 12
Van Buren, Martin, 56
Van, moving, 51
Venus de Milo, 97
Violin, 90
Vowels, 118

Wagon trains, 44
Waitress, 123
Walrus, 78
Washington: D.C., 56; George, 55, 56
Water, 37, 38
Weightlifting, 29
Whales, 84, 99
Whistler's mother, 24
Wig, 57
Wilde, Oscar, 101
William Tell, 26
Witches, 5, 11
Woodpeckers, 71
Word, 110
Worm, 105
Wrestling, mud, 52
Wright, Orville and Wilbur, 27
Wristwatch, 44

Yaks, 82
Yardwork, 66